Sabbath Meditations

John Mark Comer
and Practicing the Way

WaterBrook

WaterBrook

An imprint of the Penguin Random House Christian Publishing Group, a division of Penguin Random House LLC

1745 Broadway, New York, NY 10019

waterbrookmultnomah.com
penguinrandomhouse.com

Published in association with Yates & Yates, www.yates2.com.

Originally self-published by Practicing the Way (practicingtheway.org) in 2022.

Permission credits can be found on page 156.

Hardcover ISBN 979-8-217-15237-7
Ebook ISBN 979-8-217-15238-4

Printed in China

9 8 7 6 5 4 3 2

The authorized representative in the EU for product safety and compliance is Penguin Random House Ireland, Morrison Chambers, 32 Nassau Street, Dublin D02 YH68, Ireland. https://eu-contact.penguin.ie

BOOKMAKING TEAM: Production editor: Laura K. Wright • Managing editor: Julia Wallace • Production manager: Linnea Knollmueller • Copyeditor: Tracey Moore • Proofreader: JoLeigh Buchanan

Book and cover design by Practicing the Way

For details on special quantity discounts for bulk purchases, contact specialmarketscms@penguinrandomhouse.com.

Contents

Welcome

The Sabbath is a day like no other. In the Genesis account, we read that God "blessed the [Sabbath] day and made it holy" (2v3). The word "holy" is *qadosh* in Hebrew, and it means "unique, special, or uncommon."

The Sabbath is a day of uncommon goodness. Of what the Hebrews called shalom. It is an aftertaste of Eden—a time when all was as it was meant to be. And it is a foretaste of eternity, of "a new heaven and a new earth" (Revelation 21v1)—a day in which we anticipate and act out our glorious future as the people of God, a new community, sitting around a table to feast with King Jesus, in a world set free from the curse and made new under his good rule.

It is a day set apart.

To **stop**.
To **rest**.
To **delight**.
And to **worship**.

Without fail it is the best day of the week; the day we look forward to on Thursday, Friday, and Saturday, and we remember on Monday, Tuesday, and Wednesday.* The anchor of our week, and of our entire life with God and with our community. That's why it's on day seven, not on day three or four. It's not a "break" from our busy lives; it is the aim of our lives. On the Sabbath, we practice eternity in time.

It is holy.

But in the Ten Commandments we are commanded to "remember the Sabbath day by keeping it holy" (Exodus 20v8).

So, it is holy, but we also have to *keep* it holy.

Living in the Sabbathless culture of the West, the temptation is always to profane it, to treat it like just another day, to let it become a secularized day off.

For this reason, the Hebrew people don't talk about "practicing" Sabbath but "keeping" Sabbath. Keeping it holy, special. An entire day set apart just to rest, delight, and worship God.

May this book of meditations help you enter into the beauty of the Sabbath day and keep it holy.

—John Mark Comer
Founder of Practicing the Way

* Dan Allender, *Sabbath*

How to Use This Book

Life is a series of moments, but not all moments are created equal. Some are much, much better than others.

In order to keep the Sabbath holy, to keep it from being absorbed by the weekend, most Sabbath practitioners find it essential to develop a beginning and ending ritual to mark the passage into and out of the day. What the Hebrews called "sanctifying the day."

There is no right way to begin your day of rest and worship. The traditional Sabbath practice begins with a liturgy called the *Kiddush* (a word meaning "sanctification") and ends with the *Havdalah* ("separation"). Many people find that a light adaptation of these ancient liturgies can be enormously helpful.

To begin, you may want to follow this basic template:

- Put away your phones, devices, wallets, and/or anything that keeps you from Sabbath rest into a "Sabbath box." You may also want to write out any fears, sorrows, or unfinished tasks on little pieces of paper and prayerfully put them into the box as a way of setting them aside for the next 24 hours.
- Sit down around the table or in a comfortable, beautiful place, ideally with your community or family. You can sabbath alone, but it is best experienced with others.
- Begin a Sabbath liturgy.

A Liturgy for the Sabbath

Pause

Take a few deep, slow breaths and set your whole self before God.

Light the Candles

Begin by lighting two candles.* Then pray:

Blessed are you, O Lord our God, King of the universe, who has sanctified us by your commandments and commanded us to kindle the Sabbath lights.

May the Sabbath light which illumines our dwelling bring peace and happiness to our home. Bless us, O God, on this holy Sabbath, and cause your divine glory to shine upon us. Enlighten our darkness and guide us and all humankind, your children, toward truth and eternal light. Amen. (From the *Kiddush*)

Pour the Wine (if You Choose)

Then pray:

Come, let us welcome the Sabbath in joy and peace! Like a bride, radiant and joyous, comes the Sabbath. It brings blessings to our hearts; workday thoughts and cares are put aside. The brightness of the Sabbath light shines forth to tell that the divine spirit of love abides within our home. In that Light all our blessings are enriched, all our griefs and trials are softened. (From the *Kiddush*)

Bless the Children

Those of you who are fathers, bless your children. Look them in the eye. Put your hand on them. Smile at them. Call up all the love in your heart from the Spirit of God. And speak words of blessing, affirmation, and destiny over them.

Next, have all those present turn and bless each other. If you don't know what to say, you can simply speak this blessing: "May you be happy and at peace on this Sabbath."

Reflect on a Scripture

Reflect on a Meditation

Hold Silence

Pray Together

"Shabbat shalom!"

---

* For those with small children, ask them what the two candles represent. (They are the commands to "Remember the Sabbath" in Exodus 20 and "Observe the Sabbath" in Deuteronomy 5.)

To end, you may want to follow this basic template:

- Gather together in a comfortable, beautiful place.
- Light two candles.
- Go around the circle and share your highlights of the Sabbath.
- End in a prayer of gratitude for the Sabbath and anticipation for the next Sabbath.

***Note:** Many find great joy in beginning the Sabbath on Friday or Saturday night and moving straight from this beginning ritual into the Sabbath meal—with feasting, sharing highlights from the week, practicing gratitude, singing, and dancing.*

Stop

On the Sabbath, we stop

In Genesis 2, we see that after days of making and forming, God the creator stopped—or, in other words, he "sabbathed."

He worked for six days, and then he stopped for one.

And in doing so, God built a rhythm into the fabric of the created order for his beloved creation to follow.

Now *we too* are to work for six days and then to sabbath—to stop—for one.

But while many of us feel intuitively in our bodies an ache to stop, it seems there is a vast modern conspiracy to keep us from doing so.

"Always-on" work expectations, alarm clocks, hustle culture, smartphones—all these and more drive us to gear up, not gear down, and create a world where we go and go and never stop.

So, busyness has become a sign of social status, to the point where nearly all of us have responded to the question "How are you?" with the singular word "Busy."

And in the shadow of all that productivity, earning, and accumulating is this low-grade exhaustion that has become the new normal.

But this is not the Way of God.

To each of us in the midst of this fast-paced, frenetic, exhausted culture, there is an invitation to an age-old pattern built into creation.

To work for six days and to stop for one.

To remember we are human beings, not merely human doings.

To remember that we don't have to wait for the finish line or the elusive feeling of "enough."

To remember that we are not defined by what we do, what we have, or what others think of us; we are God's loved ones.

In this act of stopping, we are freed from inflicting on ourselves the splinters that come with moving against this God-created grain and released instead to step into the rest, delight, and worship of God that we were made for.

We live in an exhausted world, yes, but we don't have to *live exhausted.*

You, right where you are, no matter your stage of life, can step into this.

And you don't have to buy it, order it online, or earn it—all you have to do is stop.

SABBATH IS...

Sabbath is blessed.

Sabbath makes us blessed.

Sabbath is holy.

Sabbath makes us holy.

Sabbath is a command.

Sabbath is a gift.

Sabbath is a law woven into the fabric of creation by the Creator.

Sabbath is an invitation.

Sabbath is a 24-hour unit of time.

Sabbath is practicing eternity in time.

Sabbath is a day.

Sabbath is a way of being.

Sabbath is rhythm.

Sabbath is resistance.

Sabbath means we don't have to hurry, because there is nothing we have to do.

Sabbath means that "it is finished."

Sabbath means that we work from love, not for love.

Sabbath means we can rest because we are no longer slaves.

Sabbath means we must never become slave drivers.

Sabbath means that we do not need to ask, because we lack nothing.

Sabbath means that we do not need to buy, because we lack nothing.

Sabbath means that we do not need to want, because we lack nothing.

Sabbath means that we do not need to complain, because we lack nothing.

Sabbath breaks our addiction to the twin gods of accomplishment and accumulation.

Sabbath says that we are not what we do, what we have, or what others think of us.

Sabbath says we are who we are loved by.

Sabbath must be prepared for.

Sabbath must be sacrificed for.

Sabbath must be remembered.

Sabbath must be observed—guarded, protected, watched over.

Sabbath puts a wall around beauty and goodness.

Sabbath brings maturity and health.

Sabbath brings healing and deliverance.

Sabbath is not a denial of pain but a determination to move through pain into joy.

Sabbath is embracing our limits and accepting our finitude.

Sabbath shatters the illusion of control.

Sabbath reminds us that the Lord is our shepherd. Someone else is caring for us.

Sabbath says the world will get along just fine without us for a while.

Sabbath says someone else is running the universe, and he is a good king.

Sabbath is for quiet and solitude.

Sabbath is for celebration and community.

Sabbath is a day to delight in the goodness of the world.

Sabbath is a day to delight in the goodness of our lives in the world.

Sabbath is a day to delight in God.

Sabbath is a day for worship. To orient and reorient all we are back to God.

Sabbath is for God.

Sabbath is a signpost in time.

Sabbath points backward to Eden.

Sabbath points forward to the New Jerusalem.

Sabbath is a taste of heaven on earth.

Sabbath is where God is taking his people to live forever.

—Christian Dawson and John Mark Comer

REFLECTION

To keep the Sabbath means that we embrace a wholly different set of values from those of the world around us. In the first place, we embrace intentionality: we choose carefully how and why we do what we do. We live deliberately in order to embrace a quality of life that is possible only in relationship with the Lord of the Sabbath.

Second, we embrace the values of the Christian community. We spend time together with others of God's people so that the virtues of Christian character can be nourished in our own lives. We want our children to be nurtured in Christ-like qualities so that they will gladly and freely choose to participate in the community of his people.

We embrace time instead of space, people instead of things, holy happening in history instead of fate, freedom instead of a schedule. We do not have to do anything on the Sabbath day, so we are free to move as the Holy Spirit leads us, to participate in whatever opportunities the day gives. Thereby we are set free to care more deeply about others and to discover more richly who they are as fellow children of God.

In addition, we embrace giving instead of requiring. The Sabbath is a day for sharing, for gifting others in many ways, for knowing that the Lord of the Sabbath provides abundantly for us so that we can, in turn, be generous.

The Sabbath day often enables us to discover new insights into our own calling in life and to embrace that calling more thoroughly. This equips us for living out the truth of God's presence in our lives throughout the week in new ways. Finally, embracing all of these values leads to greater wholeness. To keep the Sabbath is closely connected with God's shalom, for we can experience the wholeness of his design only if we follow the orderly pattern—commanded in his Word and written into our being—for six days of work and a day of rest.

—Marva J. Dawn, *Keeping the Sabbath Wholly*

REFLECTION

At least one day in every seven, pull off the road and park the car in the garage. Close the door to the toolshed and turn off the computer. Stay home not because you are sick but because you are well. Talk someone you love into being well with you. Take a nap, a walk, an hour for lunch. Test the premise that you are worth more than what you can produce—that even if you spent one whole day of being good for nothing you would still be precious in God's sight—and when you get anxious because you are convinced that this is not so, remember that your own conviction is not required. This is a *commandment*. Your worth has already been established, even when you are not working. The purpose of the commandment is to woo you to the same truth.

—Barbara Brown Taylor, *An Altar in the World*

REFLECTION

"For the Restless Busybody"

Loving Father, why do I busy myself and run from you?

Why do I orchestrate my own self-established conditions for rest?

I feebly attempt to manipulate my environment to manufacture my own peace,

As if then, and only then, can I stop and come to quiet.

Help me surrender my illusion of control.

Remind me that there will always remain one thing unfinished—

One last errand to run, another text to respond to, one more dish in the sink.

Clinging so tightly to the satisfaction of accomplishment—

What a fragile thing to put my hope in.

Teach me to rest in the mess of my ordinary life.

Set me free from the tyranny of the undone.

Help me to love; let striving cease.

Let me trust in your faithfulness.

You are so good,

So kind.

—Bri Elam

REFLECTION

Sabbath is that one day. It is a reprieve from what you ought to do, even though the list of oughts is infinitely long and never done. Oughts are tyrants, noisy and surly, chronically dissatisfied. Sabbath is the day you trade places with them: they go in the salt mine, and you go out dancing. It's the one day when the only thing you must do is to not do the things you must. You are given permission—issued a command, to be blunt—to turn your back on all those oughts. You get to willfully ignore the many niggling things your existence genuinely depends on—and is often hobbled beneath—so that you can turn to whatever you've put off and pushed away for lack of time, lack of room, lack of breath. You get to shuck the *have-tos* and lay hold of the *get-tos*.

—Mark Buchanan, *The Rest of God*

REFLECTION

Slowly pray this descending prayer out loud together to begin your Sabbath.

Be still and know that I am God.

Be still and know that I am.

Be still and know that I.

Be still and know that.

Be still and know.

Be still and.

Be still.

Be . . .

REFLECTION

"Sabbath Poem IX" (2000)

To the abandoned fields
The trees returned and grew.
They stand and grow. Time comes
To them, time goes, the trees
Stand; the only place
They go is where they are.
These wholly patient ones
Who only stand and wait
For time to come to them,
Who do not go to time,
Stand in eternity.
They stand where they belong.
They do no wrong, and they
Are beautiful. What more
Could we have thought to ask?
Here God and man have rest.

I've gone too far toward time,

And now have come back home. . . .

I stand and wait for light

To open the dark night.

I stand and wait for prayer

To come and find me here.

—Wendell Berry, *This Day*

REFLECTION

God made us from dust. We're never too far from our origins. The apostle Paul says we're only clay pots—dust mixed with water, passed through fire. Hard, yes, but brittle too. Knowing this, God gave us the gift of Sabbath—not just as a day, but as an orientation, a way of seeing and knowing. Sabbath-keeping is a form of mending. It's mortar in the joints. Keep Sabbath, or else break too easily, and oversoon. Keep it, otherwise our dustiness consumes us, becomes us, and we end up able to hold exactly nothing.

—Mark Buchanan, *The Rest of God*

REFLECTION

To the biblical mind *menuha* is the same as happiness and stillness, as peace and harmony. . . . It is the state in which there is no strife and no fighting, no fear and no distrust. The essence of good life is *menuha*. “The Lord is my shepherd, I shall not want, He maketh me to lie down in green pastures; He leadeth me besides the still waters” (the waters of *menuhot*). In later times, *menuha* became a synonym for the life in the world to come, for eternal life.

Six evenings a week we pray: “Guard our going out and our coming in”; on the Sabbath evening we pray instead: “Embrace us with a tent of Thy peace.”

—Abraham Joshua Heschel, *The Sabbath*

REFLECTION

We stop because there are forces larger than we that take care of the universe, and while our efforts are important, necessary, and useful, they are not (nor are we) indispensable. The galaxy will somehow manage without us for this hour, this day, and so we are invited—nay, commanded—to relax, and enjoy our relative unimportance, our humble place at the table in a very large world. The deep wisdom embedded in creation will take care of things for a while.

When we breathe, we do not stop inhaling because we have taken in all the oxygen we will ever need, but because *we have all the oxygen we need for this breath.*

—Wayne Muller, "Let It Be"

REFLECTION

A psalm. A song. For the Sabbath day.

It is good to praise the LORD
 and make music to your name, O Most High,
proclaiming your love in the morning
 and your faithfulness at night,
to the music of the ten-stringed lyre
 and the melody of the harp.

For you make me glad by your deeds, LORD;
 I sing for joy at what your hands have done.
How great are your works, LORD,
 how profound your thoughts!
Senseless people do not know,
 fools do not understand,
that though the wicked spring up like grass
 and all evildoers flourish,
 they will be destroyed forever.

But you, Lord, are forever exalted.

For surely your enemies, Lord,
surely your enemies will perish;
all evildoers will be scattered.
You have exalted my horn like that of a wild ox;
fine oils have been poured on me.
My eyes have seen the defeat of my adversaries;
my ears have heard the rout of my wicked foes.

The righteous will flourish like a palm tree,
they will grow like a cedar of Lebanon;
planted in the house of the Lord,
they will flourish in the courts of our God.
They will still bear fruit in old age,
they will stay fresh and green,
proclaiming, "The Lord is upright;
he is my Rock, and there is no wickedness in him."

—Psalm 92

REFLECTION

The Sabbath is more than a break or a pause; it's a deep, profound union between humankind and the creation. It's a dynamic engagement with that unifying Spirit that connects heaven and earth. All that's sacred is united with God. This is sabbath and the deepest joy of the cosmos.

—Adapted from Abraham Joshua Heschel, *The Sabbath*

REFLECTION

"Keeping Holy"

God over our days,

As we remember this Sabbath, keep us in your holiness.

Today we stop, that we might move deeper into your invitation to life.

As we lay down our job-shaped identities, guide us through these hours in ways that honor you—and that honor your work in us.

We ready this space for you, even as you prepare a place for us.

Come, living Spirit, breathe your life into us.

We would come alive to you, O God.

Amen.

—Dan Matheson

REFLECTION

We live much of our lives producing and achieving. Sometimes, without even realizing it, we try to prove our worth by how much we get done, how much we own, or how much others notice us.

But now, we stop.

On this Sabbath day, we step off the hamster wheel. We breathe deeply and give thanks. We remember that our value comes not from what we accomplish, what we have, or what others think of us but from who we are—daughters and sons deeply loved by our Father in heaven.

This day invites us to rest in that love. To let go of striving.

As we let go, we become more aware of how fully we are known and cherished.

—Ken Shigematsu

REFLECTION

To keep a Sabbath is to give time and space on our calendar to the grace of God.

—A. J. Swoboda, *Subversive Sabbath*

REFLECTION

O God, who on this day didst
  rest from all Thy works,
grant us also Sabbath rest in Thee—
  stillness of the passions,
  calm of the mind,
and peace in the heart.
Amen.

—Strahan Coleman, inspired by Saint Basil the Great

REFLECTION

If busyness can become a kind of violence, we do not have to stretch our perception very far to see that Sabbath time—effortless, nourishing rest—can invite a healing of this violence. When we consecrate a time to listen to the still, small voices, we remember the root of inner wisdom that makes work fruitful. We remember from where we are most deeply nourished, and see more clearly the shape and texture of the people and things before us.

—Wayne Muller, "Remember the Sabbath"

REFLECTION

The table is set.

Our Sabbath candles are lit.

A meal has been prepared.

Bread has been baking. Wine is breathing.

People are gathering to feast and to pray, to bless one another with their

presence and their words. Sharing together in this sacred act where Christ is

both center and circumference.

And behind the door lies a basket of laundry unfolded.

In the drawer, a phone sits with unchecked messages.

There are emails unsent, tasks left undone.

And yet we stop.

We enter rest.

What is incomplete will remain incomplete for now.

We choose to live in the tension of all that is unfinished,

knowing that all things are held

in the loving completeness

of Father, Son, and Spirit.

—Gemma Ryan

REFLECTION

On the Sabbath we remember . . .

We remember there is a creator God. We live in his world, and it's good.

We remember there's a rhythm to creation.

We remember that we don't stop when we're finished, because we're never finished; it's never enough. We stop when the rhythm God built into our bodies says "stop."

We remember we're not what we do or what we have or what other people think of us. We are whom we are deeply loved by.

Many people fear stopping; they fear what emotions may come up—*who am I if I'm not producing or performing?* Sabbath is a weekly act of identity formation, when we each remember, *I am God's loved one.*

We remember that life with God is not a right but a gift.

We remember that the world is full of evil and injustice, yes, but it's also full of goodness and beauty and truth.

We remember that we owe it to God to be grateful and full of joy in his world.

—Adapted from Practicing the Way, *The Sabbath Practice*

REFLECTION

God has supplied us with work,

with the fruitfulness of earth

and of our labors.

Today he invites us to rest

and to trust in his providing love.

Help us, Father, to take off the yoke of our

successes and our addictions to them,

of our disappointments and the heaviness

they bring, of our worry, anxiety, and

insecurity, that we may receive gentle

Jesus, deeply resting in his tender love.

—Strahan Coleman

Rest

On the Sabbath, we rest

We all live with chronically unsatisfied desires. No matter how much we seem to get, it never feels like enough.

The Bible calls this inner disquiet "restlessness."

And one of the ways we fight against this restless ache in our hearts is through Sabbath.

In the Exodus story, before the command to sabbath is given, we read all sorts of language that shows the restlessness the Hebrews carried and came from in Egypt.

"Why are you taking the people away from their labor? Get back to your work!"

"You will not be given any straw, yet you must produce your full quota of bricks."

"Lazy! That's what you are! Lazy! That's why you whine, 'Let us go so we can worship God.'"

Pharaoh was a cruel tyrant. No matter how hard the Hebrews worked, it was never enough. They lived under the oppressive yoke of the daily quota—more, more, more.

God's command to "remember the Sabbath" is to remind the Israelites they are no longer slaves—they're in a new kingdom, ruled by a different King. There's no daily quota anymore. No taskmaster pressing in from above.

So Sabbath isn't just about a rhythm; it's about *resistance*.

And we need this kind of resistance in the modern West, where we work more than ever before, have more than ever before, and still remain unhappy.

It's Egypt all over again.

But it doesn't have to be this way.

On the Sabbath, we rest from work.

On the Sabbath, we rest from even thinking about work.

On the Sabbath, we rest from wanting and worrying.

And in doing so, we break our addiction to the twin gods of the West—achievement and accumulation.

Sabbath is a weekly declaration that Pharaoh and his army are at the bottom of the Red Sea. We are free to live in a new kingdom, under a new King.

We don't have to produce or perform or buy our way into love.

We don't have to hold our lives together or fear what lies ahead.

We can rest.

REFLECTION

Are you exhausted all the time? Waking up to your alarm clock day after day? Always in a hurry, late for the next thing, impatient with life? Do you feel haggard? Rarely your best self? Drowning under the tide of options and opportunities? Constantly trying to catch up to the ideal life that is always just out of reach? Come to me. Slow your whole life down.

Let me show you how to shoulder the weight of life with ease, even joy. Other people offer escape aplenty; I offer something more: real, true rest. Soul-level rest. Copy the details of my life, pattern the rhythm of your life after mine, and slowly but surely, I will teach you how to live with more ease and gratitude and joy than you ever thought possible.

—John Mark Comer, paraphrase of Matthew 11v28—30

REFLECTION

We step now, together, into a day of rest.

We rest from our work.

We rest from our thoughts of our work.

We rest from our wanting and worrying.

In you, Father, Son, and Holy Spirit, we come to rest.

—Adapted from Practicing the Way, *The Sabbath Practice*

REFLECTION

Resisting limits isn't new for the human race. From the very beginning we've had an animosity toward finitude and boundaries. In their rebellion, Adam and Eve wanted to be "like God." Invincible. All-sufficient. Autonomous. Limitless . . .

What if Christians were known as a countercultural community of the well-rested—people who embrace our limits with zest and even joy?

As believers we can relish sleep as not only necessary but as an embodied response to the truth of Scripture: we are finite, weak creatures who are abundantly cared for by our strong and loving Creator.

—Tish Harrison Warren, *Liturgy of the Ordinary*

REFLECTION

Most of the things we need in order to be most fully alive never come from pushing. They grow in rest.

—Mark Buchanan, *The Holy Wild*

REFLECTION

The Sabbath is God's antidote for our hurried, harried pace of life, and gives us the unhurried one-in-seven rhythm woven into the very fabric of creation. That seventh day is a space for us to enter into needed recovery (and perhaps go through the inevitable withdrawals) from the hurry, drivenness and workaholism that plague so many of our lives, families, communities and organizations. On the Sabbath, hurry becomes a vice, the exact opposite of our workaday world's way of making it a virtue.

—Alan Fadling, *An Unhurried Life*

REFLECTION

Jesus chose life on the Sabbath. He healed the sick, fed the hungry, and supported rescuing animals that fell into wells.

Sabbath is not only about stopping and resting—it's also about delight.

My friend Mark Buchanan says Sabbath is "a reprieve from what you ought to do. . . . Oughts are tyrants, noisy and surly, chronically dissatisfied. Sabbath is the day you trade places with them: they go into the salt mine, and you go out dancing."

So today, we let the "oughts" rest. The emails, the errands, the endless lists—all can wait until tomorrow. Today, we make room for what brings life and joy.

We savor pancakes. We take a slow walk under the trees. We read for pleasure, listen to music, call a friend, make something delicious, or do nothing at all—to surrender to joy.

On this Sabbath remember all of life is a gift from our Father.

—Ken Shigematsu

REFLECTION

It is difficult, but if we slow to quiet our souls
and strive to hear silence
and we use the meaty edges of our fists
to rub away the smoky film on the "mirror darkly,"
we will faintly see and feel the peace and
composed purpose on the other side.
And for a time, be enfolded with the God
who shares his harmonious will.
Leaning back in spirit like that weaned child
upon its mother.
A place of reverence and rest.
Sabbath.

—Brent Heid

REFLECTION

I asked Moshe why it was, apart from emulating the actions of the Creator, that ceasing to work on the Sabbath honored God. . . .

"What happens when we stop working and controlling nature?" he asked, peering at me over the top of his glasses. "When we don't operate machines, or pick flowers, or pluck fish from the sea, or change darkness to light, or turn wood into furniture? When we cease interfering with the world we are acknowledging that it is God's world."

—Lis Harris, *Holy Days*

REFLECTION

We are a restless people.

Restlessness is the opposite of being restful. Restfulness is one of the most primal cravings humans have. We crave rest to the point where we identify it with heaven: "Grant us eternal rest."

Today, as our lives grow more pressured, as we grow more tired, as we begin to feel burned out, we fantasize more about restfulness. We imagine a peaceful, quiet place: we see ourselves walking by a lake, watching a peaceful sunset, smoking a pipe in a rocker by the fireplace. But even in those images, we make restfulness yet another activity, something we do . . . then we return to normal life.

True restfulness, though, is a form of awareness, a way of being in life. It is living ordinary life with a sense of ease, gratitude, appreciation, peace, and prayer. We are restful when ordinary life is enough.

—Ronald Rolheiser, *The Shattered Lantern*

REFLECTION

Remember the Sabbath day by keeping it holy. Six days you shall labor and do all your work, but the seventh day is a sabbath to the Lord your God. On it you shall not do any work, neither you, nor your son or daughter, nor your male or female servant, nor your animals, nor any foreigner residing in your towns. For in six days the Lord made the heavens and the earth, the sea, and all that is in them, but he rested on the seventh day. Therefore the Lord blessed the Sabbath day and made it holy.

—Exodus 20v8—11

REFLECTION

The Sabbath commandment enjoins quietness of heart, tranquility of mind. This is holiness because here is the Spirit of God.

This is what a true holiday means: quietness and rest. Unquiet people recoil from the Holy Spirit. They love quarreling. They love argument. In their restlessness they do not allow the silence of the Lord's Sabbath to enter their lives.

Against such restlessness we are offered a kind of Sabbath in the heart. As if God were saying, "Stop being so restless; quiet the uproar in your mind. Let go of the idle fantasies that fly around in your head." God is saying, "Be still, and know that I am God" (Psalm 46v10).

But you refuse to be still. You are like the Egyptians tormented by gnats. These tiniest of flies, always restless, flying about aimlessly, swarm at your eyes, giving no rest. They are back as soon as you drive them off. Just like the futile fantasies that swarm in our minds.

Keep the commandment. Beware of this plague.

—Adapted from Saint Augustine, "Sermon 8" (on the Old Testament)

REFLECTION

"Soul Friend"

Draw me to the hearth of inner love,

Toward close fires and healing meals,

Like the frosted months gather life

And balm the soul.

Indulge me in the longing

Of taffy-stretched conversation:

Too sweet, too long, and altogether too delightful.

Put past the mere bread of daily need

And savor this banquet of joy and pleasure.

Rejoice with me in feasting fellowship!

Ride the highs of bellowed laughter

And bear with me the stomach-rising falls

That dip near despair.

Keep pace.

In step and in time to notice the coloring

Of leaves and stiffening branches.

Let us be bored to depth:

Each gravity-laden foot, sinking deeper to life

Without fear or worry but with rest.

Help me know at the beginning what we'll have

In the end: a friend.

Friendship is the victory—

Born from it, moved by it, and lost in it.

Let us savor at the beginning

What we'll know in the end: God is friendship.

—Bryan Rouanzoin

REFLECTION

In the relentless busyness of modern life, we have lost the rhythm between work and rest.

All life requires a rhythm of rest. There is a rhythm in our waking activity and the body's need for sleep. There is a rhythm in the way day dissolves into night, and night into morning. There is a rhythm as the active growth of spring and summer is quieted by the necessary dormancy of fall and winter. There is a tidal rhythm, a deep, eternal conversation between the land and the great sea. In our bodies, the heart perceptibly rests after each life-giving beat; the lungs rest between the exhale and the inhale.

We have lost this essential rhythm. Our culture invariably supposes that action and accomplishment are better than rest, that doing something—anything—is better than doing nothing. Because of our desire to succeed, to meet these ever-growing expectations, we do not rest. Because we do not rest, we lose our way. We miss the compass points that would show us where to go, we bypass the nourishment that would give us succor. We miss the quiet that would give us wisdom. We miss the joy and love born of effortless delight.

Poisoned by this hypnotic belief that good things come only through unceasing determination and tireless effort, we can never truly rest. And for want of rest, our lives are in danger.

—Wayne Muller, "Remember the Sabbath"

REFLECTION

Awaken me to rest.

I abandoned the fields you've never left

Yet you filled my storehouses with love.

I see a thousand harvests reaped

And seasons that kept changing

When I couldn't meet the muscle to winter's bone.

You were out there to see the light break,

A Father watching over countless hills

Waiting for a single son to greet the day beside.

Many things have held me inside—

Separation, sleeping through soliloquies.

There is work ahead and days beyond reach,

But all the light I missed is not behind me.

It is gathered anew every morning,

And what waits is only ever fully present

Here now, as dawn warms me into spring,

I am awakened into rest.

—Caleb Saenz

REFLECTION

By the seventh day God had finished the work he had been doing; so on the seventh day he rested from all his work. Then God blessed the seventh day and made it holy, because on it he rested from all the work of creating that he had done.

—Genesis 2v2—3

REFLECTION

Whatever you will complete or not today, rest in the only work that will never need to be done again. Rest in the fact that Jesus has done the most impossible job in the world, done it perfectly, and made it available. Take it. Enjoy it. Build your life on it. Let it change your whole view of your life and work. Use His work to put your work into perspective. Believe His work is counted as yours.

—David Murray, *The Happy Christian*

REFLECTION

> The women who had come with Him from Galilee followed after, and they observed the tomb and how His body was laid. Then they returned and prepared spices and fragrant oils. And they rested on the Sabbath according to the commandment.
>
> —Luke 23v55-56, NKJV

After the death of Jesus one would think nothing else mattered, certainly not Sabbath or rest. Heartbroken and devastated, these women believed Jesus was the Messiah, and he was dead.

They planned to go to the tomb to anoint him immediately. But there was a problem—it was the Sabbath. Wasn't this Sabbath worth breaking? To go to be with their Lord? And yet they kept it. They abided by these built-in rhythms—an invitation to rest in the midst of their deepest sorrow. They kept the command even when surely breaking it would seem justified.

They received this invitation to rest, and while they rested, Jesus conquered death. He didn't stop working. He beat the grave, paying our price, while his people sabbathed.

This reminds me that there is work that is not mine to do. That Jesus invites me to rest and let him hold all things. Whether in my highest joy or deepest grief, God gives me a weekly invitation to rest. This rest is not contingent on my accomplishments or earning of it or my satisfaction with the work I've contributed.

It's not dependent on whether or not I've finished doing everything "needed" or even how many needs around me cry out for my attention. I'm invited to rest in my plenty and my lack, my successes and my failures, in my highest contributions and my coming up short, in the midst of a thousand small undone things and even in the midst of massive needs—like caring for the body of Jesus.

Even then, God invites me to rest—to let him work perfectly and free me from the burden I feel to do the same. God invited these women to sabbath, and in their keeping that Sabbath, the Sabbath kept them until Jesus' resurrection.

God, we ask you to keep us as we keep this Sabbath, to hold all things while we relinquish them to your care this day.

—Julianne Gavin

REFLECTION

"Sabbath Poem V" (1990)

Sleep is the prayer the body prays,

Breathing in unthought faith the Breath

That through our worry-wearied days

Preserves our rest, and is our truth.

—Wendell Berry, *This Day*

REFLECTION

Today we listen to the words of Yahweh, who brought his people out of Egypt, and not the voice of Pharaoh.

Pharaoh says, "Why are you taking the people away from their labor? Get back to your work!" (Exodus 5v4).

Yahweh says, "Observe the Sabbath day by keeping it holy, as the LORD your God has commanded you" (Deuteronomy 5v12).

Pharaoh says, "They are lazy; that is why they are crying out, 'Let us go and sacrifice to our God'" (Exodus 5v8).

Yahweh says, "Six days you shall labor and do all your work, but the seventh day is a sabbath to the LORD your God. On it you shall not do any work, neither you, nor your son or daughter, nor your male or female servant, nor your ox, your donkey or any of your animals, nor any foreigner residing in your towns, so that your male and female servants may rest, as you do" (Deuteronomy 5v13—14).

Pharaoh says, "Make the work harder . . . so that they keep working" (Exodus 5v9).

Yahweh says, "Remember that you were slaves in Egypt and that the LORD your God brought you out of there with a mighty hand and an outstretched arm" (Deuteronomy 5v15).

REFLECTION

> The LORD is my shepherd, I lack nothing.
> He makes me lie down in green pastures,
> he leads me beside quiet waters,
> he refreshes my soul.
> He guides me along the right paths
> for his name's sake.
>
> —Psalm 23v1—3

We are all hapless sheep,

unsure which way to turn

or how to find eternal life;

but God is a good shepherd

and asks us to trust him with

our lives, guiding us in right

paths, calling us to quiet rest.

Good Shepherd, trustworthy and caring, we admit that we are wholly lost without you, wandering in our wildernesses afraid and in despair. Guide us this Sabbath in your right paths, correct our maligned trajectories, slow down our souls, and teach us what it means to lie in your resting waters. Amen.

—Strahan Coleman

REFLECTION

This isn't quiet time alone with God.

It is quiet time with me.

Full of anxious thoughts, to-dos, and fears,

His face I barely see.

Yet I sense him near. I hear his heart.

So peaceful and serene.

I kick and twist.

I pull and push.

No settling down it seems.

He waits patiently for his restless child,

As I strain against the sound.

The silent song of stillness.

His love song softly calming me down.

Here I find the tender start

  of

  self

  letting go.

He holds me close.

He says my name.

My mind now growing clear,

I touch his face in wonder,

As my burdens disappear.

Lighter now, they drift away,

On notes of love and grace.

His love song sung so gently,

As his Sabbath fills this space.

—Deon LaFond

REFLECTION

Without rest, we miss the rest of God: the rest he invites us to enter more fully so that we might know him more deeply. "Be still, and know that I am God." Some knowing is never pursued, only received. And for that, you need to be still.

Sabbath is both a day and an attitude to nurture such stillness. It is both time on a calendar and a disposition of the heart. It is a day we enter, but just as much a way we see. Sabbath imparts the rest of God—actual physical, mental, spiritual rest, but also the *rest* of God—the things of God's nature and presence we miss in our busyness.

—Mark Buchanan, *The Rest of God*

REFLECTION

Sabbath is a period of "trying on" God's promised completion, trying on God's future. . . . Sabbath is the inviting of all creation to be still and imagine the coming of God.

—Andrew Root, *Unlocking Mission and Eschatology in Youth Ministry*

REFLECTION

We meet dozens of people, have so many conversations. We do not feel how much energy we spend on each activity, because we imagine we will always have more energy at our disposal. This one little conversation, this one extra phone call, this one quick meeting, what can it cost? But it does cost, it drains yet another drop of our life. Then, at the end of days, weeks, months, years, we collapse, we burn out, and cannot see where it happened. It happened in a thousand unconscious events, tasks, and responsibilities that seemed easy and harmless on the surface but that each, one after the other, used a small portion of our precious life.

And so we are given a commandment: Remember the Sabbath.

—Wayne Muller, "Rest for the Weary"

REFLECTION

"Sabbath Poem X" (1979)

Whatever is foreseen in joy
Must be lived out from day to day,
Vision held open in the dark
By our ten thousand days of work.
Harvest will fill the barn; for that
The hand must ache, the face must sweat.

And yet no leaf or grain is filled
By work of ours; the field is tilled
And left to grace. That we may reap,
Great work is done while we're asleep.

When we work well, a Sabbath mood
Rests on our day, and finds it good.

—Wendell Berry, *This Day*

REFLECTION

The silence of the Sabbath allows our mind time to kick up its feet and rest. Such a move may seem contrary to our idolatry of distraction. But in that silence we will find a kind of freedom that gives us space to apply our minds to the goodness and glories of the living God.

—A. J. Swoboda, *Subversive Sabbath*

REFLECTION

Can we run with the horses? Can we run with perseverance the race set before us?

Sometimes, the greater struggle is to stop running. To slow down, entering into stillness and quietness, trusting that we are loved and valued in our resting just as much as in our working.

When we run, racing through our days with hurry and toil, we can often be oblivious to the racing of our minds, to bodies that are wound up like a machine.

When we enter stillness, our anxious thoughts are more difficult to avoid; our bodies continue to fidget with restless energy.

Could even this be a pleasing offering of worship to you, O God? Do you delight in our feeble attempts toward God speed?

As we choose to enter rest, may we be calmed and quieted like a weaned child. Made to lie down in green pastures. Led beside quiet waters. It is here that our souls are restored.

So, restore us, O God. Re-story us, O Christ. That this spirit of Sabbath might continue to indwell us even when our time of resting comes to a close.

—Gemma Ryan

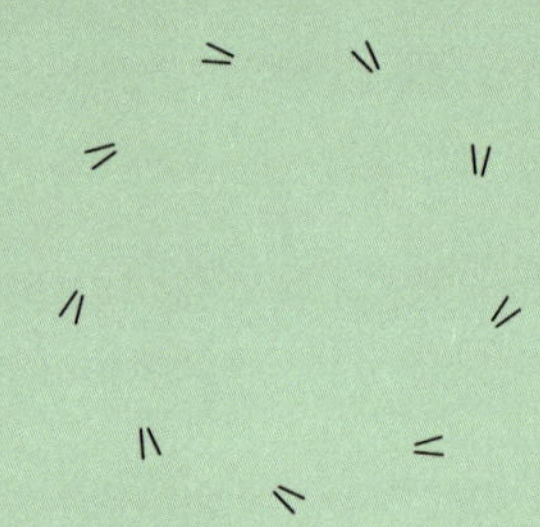

Delight

On the Sabbath, we delight

While it is true that our world is undeniably full of reasons to despair—systemic injustice, war, mass violence, crushing poverty—it is also full of reasons to delight.

All too often, the goodness and beauty of life with God in his world are eclipsed by what the New Testament writer Paul calls "the dominion of darkness" (Colossians 1v13)—the fallout of a post-Eden world.

While we can be tempted to see the darkness more than the light, Sabbath disciplines us to come out of despair and into delight.

When God rested from his creating work, embedded in the meaning of the word "rested" is this idea: that "God delighted in all his work."

Sabbath is therefore meant to be a discipline of celebration and a delivery mechanism for joy.

It's a day to allow our minds to focus on all that is "very good" in the earth. To curate a view of the world, with special attention to the good, beautiful, and true.

And above all, to delight in God himself. Not just to believe in him, learn from him, or obey him—though those are good—but to truly delight in him.

But this kind of delighting in God and his world must be a discipline.

Because often on the Sabbath—in the quiet and the space—instead of finding delight, we find there waiting for us all the other feelings we've been burying all week.

And just the reality of Sabbath being a weekly rhythm means we will sabbath in seasons of joy and seasons of lament.

But the invitation to sabbath remains the same.

When it feels more like winter than summer.

When we feel behind, not caught up.

When we sense more absence than presence from God.

Though some Sabbaths may feel like we are not stepping away from darkness but stepping into the day with it, God awaits us there.

And he is the only one who can teach us how to truly live the apostle Paul's words—to "rejoice in the Lord always" (Philippians 4v4).

REFLECTION

The Sabbath is an invitation to enter delight. The Sabbath, when experienced as God intended, is the best day of our lives. Without question or thought, it is the best day of the week. It is the day we anticipate on Wednesday, Thursday, and Friday—and the day we remember on Sunday, Monday, and Tuesday. Sabbath is the holy time where we feast, play, dance, have sex, sing, pray, laugh, tell stories, read, paint, walk, and watch creation in its fullness. Few people are willing to enter the Sabbath and sanctify it, to make it holy, because a full day of delight and joy is more than most people can bear in a lifetime, let alone a week.

—Dan Allender, *Sabbath*

REFLECTION

"If you keep your feet from breaking the Sabbath
    and from doing as you please on my holy day,
if you call the Sabbath a delight
    and the LORD's holy day honorable,
and if you honor it by not going your own way
    and not doing as you please or speaking idle words,
then you will find your joy in the LORD,
    and I will cause you to ride in triumph on the heights
        of the land
    and to feast on the inheritance of your father Jacob."
For the mouth of the LORD has spoken.

—Isaiah 58v13—14

REFLECTION

The Sabbath is a day to delight.

In God's world.

In our life in God's world.

And in God himself.

REFLECTION

> He brought me out into a spacious place;
> he rescued me because he delighted in me.
> —Psalm 18v19

In the creation story of Genesis 2, God forms the heavens and the earth and places humankind in the Garden of Eden. In Hebrew, the word "Eden" means "delight." Our first home was a Garden of Delight. Each week, Sabbath offers us a homecoming—a gentle return to the joyful place of our being and becoming, where life is received as a gift, not carried as a burden.

In the pace and pressure of contemporary life, delight is often lost—swallowed up by the pursuit of entertainment or pleasure. But true delight is something deeper and far more nourishing. Developmental psychologist Dan Hughes writes, "Only the experience of being delighted in can create a sense of being delightful, and only those who sense they are delightful can truly delight in others." Delight shapes our sense of self. We learn to delight because we've come to know we are delighted in.

On this Sabbath day, may you rest in the delight of your heavenly Father. May his delight wash over you and color every moment of this glorious gift of life.

—Bryan Rouanzoin

REFLECTION

Lord, you are like honey to the soul,
and your Spirit is like warm oil
  that soothes the heart.
When we taste your sweetness,
all bitterness is turned away.
Our whole being melts like wax
  before the fire of your love.

May it be so in us this Sabbath
and forevermore.
Amen.

—Strahan Coleman, inspired by Mechthild of Magdeburg

REFLECTION

Observing the Sabbath gives us the opportunity to be as careful as we can to fill our lives with beauty and to share beauty with the world around us. When we observe a day especially set apart for beauty, all the rest of life is made more beautiful. . . .

In a larger sense, the whole practice of Sabbath keeping makes me feel more beautiful. As I spend the day reflecting on the character of God, I am overwhelmed by his love for me. As I feast upon his goodness in all its beautiful forms, I realize more profoundly that I am a special part of his creation and designed especially for his purposes in a uniquely beautiful way.

—Marva J. Dawn, *Keeping the Sabbath Wholly*

REFLECTION

Sabbath gives us a sanctuary in time.

By entering rest, we express our love for God—not through effort but through trust. While we pause from work, we trust God continues to hold our world and care for us.

In the Hebrew imagination, as Eugene Peterson notes, each day begins at sundown. Rest comes first, not last. We begin in stillness, not striving.

As we sleep, God goes on creating: dew covering the grass, leaves unfolding in the quiet of night, rosebuds swelling in the dark. We awaken to beauty we did not make. This is grace. God does not sleep, so we can.

From this place of rest, we will return to our work not as human doings but as human beings.

We are defined not by what we produce but by our belovedness.

—Ken Shigematsu

REFLECTION

Today, we were slow enough to delight in small moments of beauty and wonder. The innocent laughter of a child, the scent of rain, the color of the sky. We were still enough to feel a light breeze on our cheeks and hear the exquisite soundscape that so often evades our notice. We savored the taste of coffee, the warmth of the sun on our skin, a heartfelt conversation with someone we love.

Creation sings. Beauty abounds. All of it pointing to the One who made it and sustains it with careful attention and tender affection. Today, once again, we taste and see how good you are and marvel at the magnitude of your love for everything you have made. It is our delight to be loved by you and to love you in return. We rest happily in your gracious care. In quietness and trust is our strength.

—Gemma Ryan

REFLECTION

"Beauty"

> It has become the habit of our times to mistake glamour for beauty. . . . Glamour . . . has but a single flicker. In contrast, the Beautiful offers us an invitation to order, coherence and unity. When these needs are met, the soul feels at home in the world.
> (John O'Donohue)

Each Sabbath, and in every moment of true, soulful presence, we are gently called back to our place of belonging with God. In the rush of daily demands—whether urgent or mundane—we are easily pulled away and forget where we are most at home.

Beauty is as essential to our life with God as prayer or devotion. Not as a replacement but as a necessary companion. When our gaze is fixed on the goodness and grace of God—when our pace begins to match his—we start to see again. We begin to hear again. Worship rises around us in unexpected places: Every bush burns with divine fire, every sunset offers a benediction, and music fills creation with the glory of God.

This Sabbath, behold the good and the beautiful. Let true beauty recalibrate your senses—tuning your eyes and ears to long for more than the glamour and efficiency of modern life. Let it become a thousand reminders of the loving Creator who paints the world with splendor and sings over you with delight.

—Bryan Rouanzoin

REFLECTION

The Christian mystic Meister Eckhart once said that if the only prayer we ever prayed in this life was “thank you,” it would be enough.

Just to be is a blessing. Just to live is holy.

—Abraham Joshua Heschel, “No Religion Is an Island”

REFLECTION

Anyone who has ever tasted of true delight—as the Creator intended for the creation—knows there is a chasm of difference between delight and hedonism or simple pleasure.

Delight is meant to draw your whole being to God in gratitude and joy; pleasure is just trying to make your body feel good. You don't walk away from pleasure feeling profound gratitude; you just walk away wanting more pleasure.

And what makes the Sabbath a day of joy isn't just good food, conversation around a table with family and friends, and time off work. It is God himself, the Trinitarian community at the center of the universe who radiates joy.

He is what we crave deep in our beings.

—Adapted from Practicing the Way, *The Sabbath Practice*

REFLECTION

"Before Time Began"

I have loved you since before you took your first breath.

Like a feather floating softly in the wind,

I waited.

Hovering as you first drew air into your lungs,

waiting,

ready to pour love into you.

I have loved you since before you opened your eyes.

Like a beam of sunlight hiding behind a cloud,

I waited.

Piercing through as your lids began to flutter,

waiting,

ready to fill you with light.

I have loved you since before you could hear my voice.

Like delicate fingers suspended over the strings of a harp,

I waited.

Releasing my whispers as your ears first took in sound,

waiting,

ready to speak life over you.

I have loved you, my darling, with the deepest of love.

One that knows no beginning

or end.

Before any spark in the universe,

before any flicker of light in the depths of darkness,

before time began,

I named you.

I called you mine.

This is the love

above all love,

above all love.

I have loved you all along.

—Jamie Phear

REFLECTION

Shabbat is like nothing else. Time as we know it does not exist during these twenty-four hours, and the worries of the week soon fall away. A feeling of joy appears. The smallest object, a leaf or a spoon, shimmers in a soft light, and the heart opens. Shabbat is a meditation of unbelievable beauty.

—Nan Fink Gefen, *Stranger in the Midst*

REFLECTION

"Learning to Notice"

Captured in its cadence, seduced in stanza 1
To see the world through silk-spun grace.
Pulling at the thread of every color-laced snapshot,
There was something irreducible.
Even muted black and whites began to cry
With colorful tongues of fire,
And the burning bushes began to sing around me—
A chorus of their calling.

And somehow the meter, at first
At odds with my restless pulse,
Pulled me deep within its orbit,
Steadying some inner rhythm
With the gravity of wonder.

Like a pilgrim or transplant, plucked from bland maps,
Some other land, a storyless life,
And now planted in the nourishing gaze of a Painter's eye.

Framed through one beholding vision and not merely a brush.

Paint is merely the voice of this telling.

The story was born before the artist ever dreamed,

Before the poet ever speaks.

—Bryan Rouanzoin

REFLECTION

Days pass and the years vanish, and we walk sightless among miracles. Lord, fill our eyes with seeing and our minds with knowing; let there be moments when Your Presence, like lightning, illumines the darkness in which we walk.

Help us to see, wherever we gaze, that the bush burns unconsumed.

And we, clay touched by God, will reach out for holiness, and exclaim in wonder:

How filled with awe is this place, and we did not know it!

—Rabbi Chaim Stern, *Gates of Prayer: The New Union Prayerbook*

REFLECTION

God has established a created order full of excellent and good things, and it follows naturally that as we give our attention to those things we will be happy. That is God's appointed way to joy. If we think we will have joy only by praying and singing psalms, we will be disillusioned. But if we fill our lives with simple, good things and constantly thank God for them, we will be joyful, that is, full of joy. . . .

The decision to set the mind on the higher things of life is an act of the will. That is why celebration is a Discipline. It is not something that falls on our heads. It is the result of a consciously chosen way of thinking and living.

—Richard Foster, *Celebration of Discipline*

REFLECTION

The Sabbath comes every seven days to remind us of the goodness of life with God in all the seasons of our lives, including the ones that don't feel very good.

Unlike other spiritual disciplines, the timing of Sabbath is set by God himself, not by our own inner spiritual clocks that tell us the need of the hour. Sabbath comes at the end of a great week and at the end of a lousy one. When we finished all our to-do list and when we're woefully behind. In summer and in winter. When all is well and when life is falling apart. To remind us it's okay that we're not okay.

In those seasons of the dark night, when our prayers are unanswered, our dreams over, and we feel God's absence more than his presence, the Sabbath comes, and with it a sense of peace, of trust in God—despite our circumstances, not because of them. Teaching us to delight and even be happy in all the seasons of our lives. Or as Paul said, to "rejoice in the Lord always" (Philippians 4v4).

—John Mark Comer

REFLECTION

For six days a week we toil with the world, reaping fruit by the sweat of our brow, but on the Sabbath, we attend to the seed of eternity planted within our hearts. While the world demands our labor, our souls belong to another.

—Adapted from Abraham Joshua Heschel, *The Sabbath*

REFLECTION

Delight is not denial of pain; it's determination to move through pain, courageously and honestly and patiently, and into joy.

Often on the Sabbath, we have space in the quiet to breathe, and in that space, whatever feelings we've been running away from all week long catch up to us.

We don't need to fight this "Sabbath sadness" or let it discourage us, as if "Sabbath isn't working"; rather, we need to let it pass over us like a wave.

On the Sabbath, we do our best to set aside all the sad things in our lives, to just let them be, for a day.

Just for this day.

—Adapated from Practicing the Way, *The Sabbath Practice*

REFLECTION

"Sabbath Poem XVII" (2012)

After the long weeks

when the heat curled the leaves

and the air thirsted, comes

a morning after rain, cool

and bright. The leaves uncurl,

the pastures begin again

to grow, the animals and the birds

rejoice. If tonight the world ends, we'll have had this day.

—Wendell Berry, *This Day*

REFLECTION

The highest compliment someone can give to a gift giver is to thoroughly enjoy the gift. The highest compliment we can give to God, our creator, is to thoroughly enjoy the gift of life. . . . The best way to pay for a beautiful moment is to enjoy it.

—Ronald Rolheiser, "Say 'Thank You' by Enjoying the Gift"

REFLECTION

Puritan sabbaths that eliminated play were a disaster. Secular sabbaths that eliminate prayer are worse. Sabbath-keeping involves both playing and praying. The activities are alike enough to share the same day and different enough to require each other for a complementary wholeness.

—Eugene Peterson, *Working the Angles*

REFLECTION

Lord of heaven and earth, glorious God who knows and sees all we do and need, we honor you with all our beings, lately in our working for the good of your kingdom and now in the rest of your loving presence. May this Sabbath be full of your joy, your love, and your stillness, that all creation may see your goodness in our midst and that we may know it very well. Amen.

—Strahan Coleman

REFLECTION

The happiness of heaven is the constant keeping of the Sabbath. Heaven is called a Sabbath, to make those who have Sabbaths long for heaven, and those who long for heaven love Sabbaths.

—Attributed to Philip Henry

REFLECTION

We enter delight only as we gaze equally and simultaneously at creation and redemption, in spite of the darkness that surrounds us and constantly clamors to be truer than God.

—Dan Allender, *Sabbath*

REFLECTION

"Sabbath Joy"

Joy Giver, what good gift is not from you?

Today, help us know honest delight in your presence.

You have our attention.

Lead us to enjoy you more deeply—and to believe that you enjoy us.

In our weariness, equip us with the strength your joy provides.

Meet the real disappointments of our lives with your real delight.

On this day of renewal, may we build the storehouses of our happiness in you

So that your joy may be at home in us.

Amen.

—Dan Matheson

REFLECTION

They that have delight in the Sabbath of God, shall find delight in the God of the Sabbath.

—John Wells, *The Practical Sabbatarian*

REFLECTION

"The Beginning"

It began with death

As all great things do.

As a mother coming undone,

  Apart at the seams,

    At least it seems,

But what living thing could pass so close

  To death

And "birth" be its given name?

Then a cry springs out from some place unseen:

  Appearing,

    Emerging,

      Untethering

From this testament of life

And becoming "life" still so un-formed.

Still this gentle form that all eyes move toward,

Like some heavenly dense gravity,

Inescapably pulling on us

  And drawing from us:

Delight.

This sense oft forgotten,

Left lost in worn boxes

With wedding shoes

And recollected hues,

Until we unwittingly awake

To scour the closets and remind ourselves

Through spine-tingling cross-legged curiosity:

We wore the scuffs

Without care

And danced wildly through fear

To arrive in the music and grow in the movement.

How we learn to settle is the last mystery,

The last death that must be revived:

That our hearts house the memory of rhythm

Even old joints can reclaim

With soft-tapping toes

And un-stiffening elbows.

Then with the sheer force of falling,

We crash through

The surface

And begin again.

—Bryan Rouanzoin

REFLECTION

Sabbath is about so much

more than rest from our work.

It's an opportunity to take

stock of, and renew, our

delight in God.

Today we thank you for the goodness of Sabbath, God,

and acknowledge that the true gift of stopping isn't bodily rest;

it's the renewing of a vital love for you and our delighting

in the joy and kindness you offer every one of us.

—Strahan Coleman

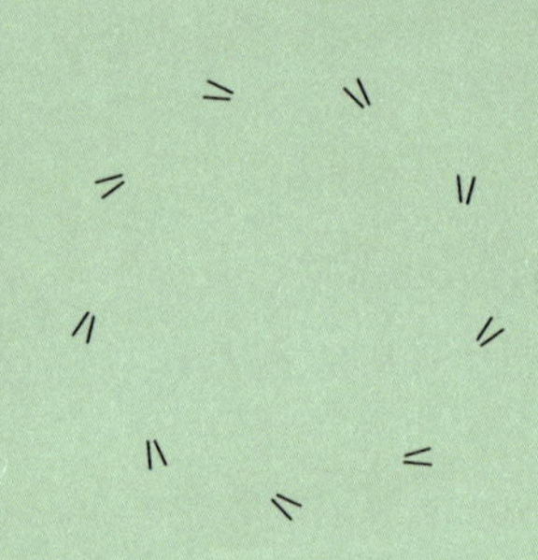

Worship

On the Sabbath, we worship

God has made the Sabbath holy—meaning it is uniquely "set apart."

The creator God has made not just a holy place for himself but also a holy day.

The entire cosmos is God's temple—there is nowhere that he is not. And on this day, set apart for himself, we choose to be awakened and enlivened to the reality of his presence all around us.

Yes, the Sabbath is a day to stop, rest, and refill our tanks.

But above all, it's a day to contemplate the good news that God has given us his life in Jesus and that it is our joy to give our lives back to him in worship.

We won't always arrive at the Sabbath day feeling like we've fully given our lives back to him in worship all week long.

Perhaps some weeks, we'll have brought our worship elsewhere—taking our internal aches to other things, misdiagnosing our longing for God as a desire for something else.

This makes the Sabbath a gift to our drifting selves.

A day to re-attune our hearts to God.

To step away from the many false and invisible gods around us that overpromise and underdeliver and to remember who is truly worthy of our worship.

With worship at its center, the Sabbath points ahead, preparing us for eternity.

For a day when God will make the fullness of his reign and his rule visible to all and worship will be our eternal response.

On the Sabbath, we practice for this day.

So, we break from our work to rest and to delight.

To enjoy a well-cooked meal with friends and family.

To read some heartfelt poetry.

To meander through an art museum.

To listen to an old record.

To go for a walk in nature.

Or whatever our Sabbath may hold.

But most importantly, we treat the day as holy—as a day uniquely set apart for God.

And we worship him.

REFLECTION

I know what it's like to rest for hours until I have the energy to delight in something—good food, a good book, a leisurely walk, a long-awaited conversation with someone I love. I know what it's like to feel joy and hope and peace flow back into my body and soul though I had thought it might never come again. I know what it's like to see my home and my children through the sabbath eyes of enjoyment. I know what it's like to have rest turn into delight, and delight turn into gratitude, and gratitude into worship.

—Ruth Haley Barton, *Sacred Rhythms*

REFLECTION

To keep the Sabbath is a great act of faith in King Jesus. It is more than agreeing with or liking the gospel as belief and doctrine; it is embodying the gospel in time and space. It is believing, responding to, and living the gospel with our bodies, money, habits, food, emotions, work, possessions, desires, rhythms, relationships, schedules, and time.

To keep Sabbath is to announce that we were once dead in sins but are now free in grace, once prisoners of hell but now citizens of heaven, once slaves to work but now free to rest, once controlled by the flesh but now led by the Spirit.

To keep Sabbath is to use every part of our lives to declare that Jesus is God and man, lord and savior, restorer and redeemer, teacher and king.

To keep Sabbath is to actually live into what God has done, is doing, and will do. It is to announce that Jesus did die, is alive, and is coming again and that we too have died, have been made alive, and will one day be raised to life.

To keep Sabbath is to step into resurrection life.

To keep Sabbath is to take to heart and lifestyle Jesus' words "It is finished" (John 19v30).

To keep Sabbath is to live into Jesus' rest for our souls. Therefore, to keep Sabbath is a great act of faith in King Jesus.

—Christian Dawson

REFLECTION

One Sabbath Jesus was going through the grainfields, and as his disciples walked along, they began to pick some heads of grain. The Pharisees said to him, "Look, why are they doing what is unlawful on the Sabbath?"

He answered, "Have you never read what David did when he and his companions were hungry and in need? In the days of Abiathar the high priest, he entered the house of God and ate the consecrated bread, which is lawful only for priests to eat. And he also gave some to his companions."

Then he said to them, "The Sabbath was made for man, not man for the Sabbath. So the Son of Man is Lord even of the Sabbath."

Another time Jesus went into the synagogue, and a man with a shriveled hand was there. Some of them were looking for a reason to accuse Jesus, so they watched him closely to see if he would heal him on the Sabbath. Jesus said to the man with the shriveled hand, "Stand up in front of everyone."

Then Jesus asked them, "Which is lawful on the Sabbath: to do good or to do evil, to save life or to kill?" But they remained silent.

He looked around at them in anger and, deeply distressed at their stubborn hearts, said to the man, "Stretch out your hand." He stretched it out, and his hand was completely restored.

—Mark 2v23—3v5

REFLECTION

For six days, we have labored in homes, schools, office buildings, and institutions. We have dedicated those many hours to hard work and creative intention, doing our best to steward well the gift of work in our hands.

Lord of the Sabbath, we hear now your invitation to enter into rest, and we receive your gift with hearts full of thankfulness. The entire cosmos is held in your hands, and with kindness and mercy, you offer us a chance to take our hands off our little piece of this earth and watch as the world keeps spinning without us.

Increase our attentiveness to the work you are doing all around us even when we are at rest. Enlarge our gratitude, deepen our trust, and release our need to control. Teach us how to live freely and lightly. May we learn to see Sabbath not as an escape from our ordinary lives but as a foretaste of our eternal future.

—Gemma Ryan

REFLECTION

Sabbath keeping is not a condition of getting into heaven; it's . . . a condition that heaven is in [when] you get there.

—Matthew Sleeth

REFLECTION

Unless one learns how to relish the taste of Sabbath while still in this world, unless one is initiated in the appreciation of eternal life, one will be unable to enjoy the taste of eternity in the world to come. . . .

The essence of the world to come is Sabbath eternal, and the seventh day in time is an example of eternity.

—Abraham Joshua Heschel, *The Sabbath*

REFLECTION

Sabbath is a signpost in time.

It points backward to creation and forward to new creation.

It is an aftertaste of Eden and a foretaste of the New Jerusalem.

On the Sabbath, we live as we did in the garden and as we will in the new heavens and new earth.

We also look forward to the day when God's kingdom will come in all its fullness and our once-a-week Sabbaths will be transformed into an eternal Sabbath feast in God's perfect presence.

—Marva J. Dawn, *Keeping the Sabbath Wholly*

REFLECTION

Our citizenship is in heaven. Between now and then, here and there, we live as sojourners, Bedouins, exiles, tent dwellers. There is always a little sand in the sheets. There is always a sense that *over there* is better than right here. If ever we achieved perfect Sabbath here, unbroken rest and restfulness, then the eternal rest that Sabbath hints at would become irrelevant.

God lets us groan now to woo us heavenward. He gives us rest here, but not enough to fully satisfy, just enough to keep us in the race. With rest he mixes restlessness. . . .

Sabbath is for rest. But it is also a good opportunity to point our restlessness heavenward.

—Mark Buchanan, *The Rest of God*

REFLECTION

There remains, then, a Sabbath-rest for the people of God; for anyone who enters God's rest also rests from their works, just as God did from his. Let us, therefore, make every effort to enter that rest.

—Hebrews 4v9—11

REFLECTION

Lord,

We come gathered,

A working people

Drawn to your stillness, attracted to your rest.

We petition not,

Only seized with expectation to delight in your consuming majesty.

We worship you now as we enter the heavens present,

Until you call us back to partnership,

Gazing with pains toward that glorious day.

—Dekota Johnson

REFLECTION

Intimacy with God cannot be rushed. . . . We cannot enjoy the presence of God if we are always looking at our watches. That is why keeping the Sabbath is so important—because on that day we never wear our watches at all.

—Marva J. Dawn, *Keeping the Sabbath Wholly*

REFLECTION

"Sabbath Poem III" (2001)

Ask the world to reveal its quietude—

not the silence of machines when they are still,

but the true quiet by which birdsongs,

trees, bellworts, snails, clouds, storms

become what they are, and are nothing else.

—Wendell Berry, *This Day*

REFLECTION

In some ways, the whole point of Exodus was Sabbath. *Let my people go,* became God's rallying cry, *that they might worship me.* At the heart of liberty—of being let go—is worship. But at the heart of worship is rest—a stopping from all work, all worry, all scheming, all fleeing—to stand amazed and thankful before God and *his* work. There can be no real worship without true rest.

—Mark Buchanan, *The Rest of God*

REFLECTION

Living God, who is perfect stillness and peace, we enter your rest this Sabbath, trusting that in all our not-doing, you are more than enough, and that in our abiding in your quiet love, we will bring you perfect glory, becoming more like you. Amen.

—Strahan Coleman

REFLECTION

As we enter the Sabbath, we are invited to worship—coming together as God's people to pray, sing, listen to God's words, and immerse ourselves in the presence of our Creator. Worship is not just a ritual; it's an opportunity to orient our lives away from ourselves and toward Jesus. He calls to us, offering rest: "Come to me, all you who are weary and burdened, and I will give you rest. Take my yoke upon you and learn from me, for I am gentle and humble in heart, and you will find rest for your souls" (Matthew 11v28–29).

Worship is essential to Sabbath; it is at the heart of our rhythm of life. When we turn to God, we are reminded that our true identity is not defined by what we do, what we have, or what others think of us but by the glorious fact that we are beloved children of God. As we worship, we quiet the restless inner noise, let go of self-condemnation, and renew our vision of God's deep love for us. In this space, we find the true rest we long for—rest for our bodies and our souls.

—Ken Shigematsu

REFLECTION

"Sabbath as Holy Ground"

The place where you are standing is holy ground.
—Exodus 3v5

God, sometimes we are afraid to look at you—

aware of the costly implications of coming close.

And we are afraid to be seen.

Look upon our vulnerabilities and our self-protective strategies

with your compassionate concern.

We come to you, the always-present One,

asking for grace to recognize your nearness.

Speak your name over us today.

Transform this space into holy ground.

Amen.

—Dan Matheson

REFLECTION

All week long, the false gods of the world lure us out of our circle around God in a kind of orbital decay, invisible yet pulling us down. They all promise us rest—and a sense of joy and satisfaction. Yet all they give is the weariness and emptiness of soul the Western world has honed to perfection.

On the Sabbath, we come back to what the Quakers called our "holy center" in God, this point deep within all of us who have been baptized, where we are "in Christ," where our spirit is in communion with his spirit, where we're not even sure who's who anymore—where we draw on the life at the heart of the Trinity itself. And give our lives back in return.

The Sabbath is a day for worship.

—Adapted from Practicing the Way, *The Sabbath Practice*

REFLECTION

Salvation is more than works.

It is stillness and quietness

and a gentle soul shaped not

only by what it does but also in

whom it loves and abides.

This Sabbath we return to you, Father,

from our distracted thoughts, our work,

and other-focused living, that we may

glory in your quiet fire and live always

from the safety of your trustworthy love.

—Strahan Coleman

REFLECTION

Shabbat comes with its own holiness; we enter not simply a day, but an atmosphere. . . . Strict adherence to the laws regulating Sabbath observance doesn't suffice; the goal is creating the Sabbath as a foretaste of paradise. . . . Each Shabbat prepares us for that experience: "Unless one learns how to relish the taste of Sabbath . . . one will be unable to enjoy the taste of eternity in the world to come."

—Susannah Heschel, introduction to
Abraham Joshua Heschel, *The Sabbath*

REFLECTION

The Sabbath is a means by which we step away from our overwork, overconsumption, and over-activity and enter into what Jesus called "the kingdom (or reign) of God."

It's a day when God's will is done on earth as it is in heaven.

—Adapted from Practicing the Way, *The Sabbath Practice*

REFLECTION

[The Sabbath] is the queen of all days, the day in which division, destitution, and death are put aside to celebrate our union with God, the abundance of his love, and the wild hope of the coming kingdom. It is a day of holy fiction, a day when the promise of God is fulfilled on a stage where we write the script and take the roles we most want to act for his glory.

—Dan Allender, *Sabbath*

May the God of rest

fill you with his

peace and presence

as you rest in him.

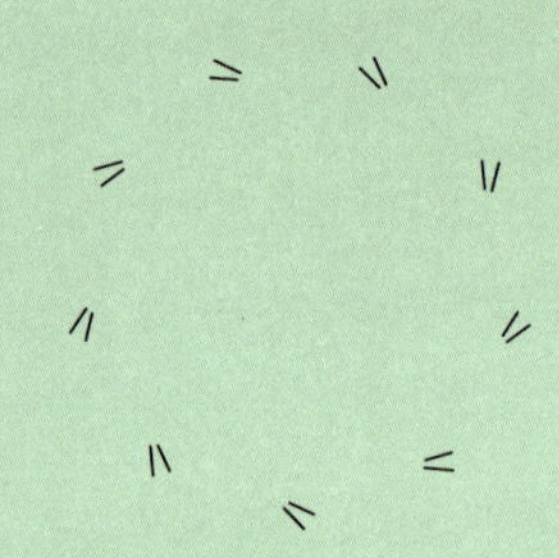

Appendix

Ideas for Stop

- Turn off all your devices.
- Take a full digital Sabbath.
- Close your email.
- Put away your to-do list.
- Refrain from running errands.
- Pause chores.
- Leave your dishes in the sink.
- Premake your food.
- Refuse any talk of work.
- Sit in silence.
- Breathe.

Ideas for Rest

- Sleep.
- Nap.
- Eat a good meal.
- Take a leisurely walk.
- Start a fire.
- Read a book.
- Stare out the window.
- Sit outside.
- Make tea.
- Savor rituals.
- Refrain from buying or selling.
- Be with your family.
- Be with your friends.

Ideas for Delight

- Eat your favorite treat—pancakes or doughnuts or that matcha latte.
- Have a dance party.
- Play music.
- Get coffee with your best friend.
- Make love to your spouse.
- Take a walk.
- Nap.
- Open a good bottle of wine.
- Do your nails or favorite self-care activity.
- Go fishing or surfing or swimming.
- Be in nature.
- Watch the sun rise or set.
- Make a fire.
- Read fiction or poetry.
- Sing.
- Go to an art museum.
- Go on a picnic in a beautiful park.
- Play a game.

Ideas for Worship

- Pray the psalms.
- Go to church.
- Listen to worship music.
- Visit a cathedral.
- Take a walk in a park or nature preserve.
- Journal your heart to God.
- Read Scripture.
- Sing.
- Read a devotional classic.
- Give thanks.
- Watch the sunrise/sunset.
- Read poetry.

Recommended Reading

01 *The Sabbath*
by Abraham Joshua Heschel

02 *Keeping the Sabbath Wholly*
by Marva J. Dawn

03 *Subversive Sabbath*
by A. J. Swoboda

04 *Sabbath*
by Dan Allender

05 *The Ruthless Elimination of Hurry*
by John Mark Comer

About Practicing the Way

Sabbath Meditations is a resource from Practicing the Way—a simple, beautiful way to integrate formation into your church or small group.

Practicing the Way is a crowdfunded nonprofit. All our resources are completely free thanks to the generosity of The Circle, an online community of monthly givers who partner with us to see the spiritual formation movement integrated into the Western church.

To run a practice, join The Circle, or find out more, visit **practicingtheway.org/give**.

Permissions

Grateful acknowledgment is made to the following for permission to reprint the following material:

Bantam Books, an imprint of Random House, a division of Penguin Random House LLC: excerpt(s) from *Sabbath: Restoring the Sacred Rhythm of Rest* by Wayne Muller, copyright © 1999 by Wayne Muller. Used by permission of Bantam Books, an imprint of Random House, a division of Penguin Random House LLC. All rights reserved.

Counterpoint Press c/o The Permissions Company, LLC: ["After the long weeks'], ["Whatever is foreseen in joy"], ["Ask the world to reveal its quietude—"], and excerpts from ["I've come down from the sky"] from *This Day: Collected and New Sabbath Poems 1979—2012*, copyright © 1979, 2000, 2012 by Wendell Berry; excerpt from ["The body in the invisible"] from *This Day: Collected and New Sabbath Poems 1979—2012.* Copyright © 1990 by Wendell Berry. Used by permission of The Permissions Company, LLC on behalf of Counterpoint Press, counterpointpress.com.

Dekota Johnson, MDiv: Sabbath meditation by Dekota Johnson. Used by permission of the author.

Deon LaFond: Sabbath mediation by Deon LaFond. Used by permission of the author.

HarperCollins Christian Publishing: excerpt from *The Rest of God* by Mark Buchanan, copyright © 2006 by Mark Buchanan. Used by permission of HarperCollins Christian Publishing. www.harpercollinschristian.com.

William B. Eerdmans Publishing Company: excerpt from *Keeping the Sabbath Wholly: Ceasing, Resting, Embracing, Fasting* by Marva J. Dawn, copyright © 1989 by Wm. B. Eerdmans Publishing Company. Used by permission of the publisher; all rights reserved.

Bibliography

Allender, Dan. *Sabbath: The Ancient Practices.* Thomas Nelson, 2010.

Barton, Ruth Haley. *Sacred Rhythms: Arranging Our Lives for Spiritual Transformation.* InterVarsity, 2006.

Berry, Wendell. "After the long weeks," "Whatever is foreseen in joy," "Ask the world to reveal its quietude," and excerpts from "I've come down from the sky" and "The body in the invisible," from *This Day: Collected and New Sabbath Poems 1979—2012.* Copyright © 1979, 2000, 2012 by Wendell Berry.

Buchanan, Mark. *The Holy Wild: Trusting in the Character of God.* Multnomah, 2005.

Buchanan, Mark. *The Rest of God: Restoring Your Soul by Restoring Sabbath.* Thomas Nelson, 2006.

Dawn, Marva J. *Keeping the Sabbath Wholly: Ceasing, Resting, Embracing, Feasting.* Eerdmans, 1989.

Fadling, Alan. *An Unhurried Life: Following Jesus' Rhythms of Work and Rest.* InterVarsity, 2024.

Fink Gefen, Nan. *Stranger in the Midst: A Memoir of Spiritual Discovery.* Basic, 1997.

Foster, Richard. *Celebration of Discipline: The Path to Spiritual Growth.* Special anniversary ed. HarperOne, 2018.

Harris, Lis. *Holy Days: The World of a Hasidic Family.* Simon and Schuster, 1985.

Heschel, Abraham Joshua. "No Religion Is an Island." In *Moral Grandeur and Spiritual Audacity: Essays,* ed. Susannah Heschel. Farrar, Straus and Giroux, 1996.

Heschel, Abraham Joshua. *The Sabbath.* Farrar, Straus and Giroux, 2005.

Millgram, Abraham, ed. *The Sabbath Anthology.* University of Nebraska Press, 2018.

Muller, Wayne. "Remember the Sabbath," "Rest for the Weary," and "Let It Be" from *Sabbath: Restoring the Sacred Rhythm of Rest.* Bantam, 1999.

Murray, David. *The Happy Christian: Ten Ways to Be a Joyful Believer in a Gloomy World.* Nelson, 2015.

Peterson, Eugene. *Working the Angles: The Shape of Pastoral Integrity.* Eerdmans, 1989.

Rolheiser, Ronald. *The Shattered Lantern: Rediscovering a Felt Presence of God.* PublishDrive, 2005.

Rolheiser, Ronald. "Say 'Thank You' by Enjoying the Gift." February 6, 1995. https://ronrolheiser.com/say-thank-you-by-enjoying-the-gift.

Root, Andrew. *Unlocking Mission and Eschatology in Youth Ministry.* Zondervan, 2013.

Sleeth, Matthew. *Grace Enough Podcast.* Hosted by Amber Cullum. Episode 67, "Dr. Matthew Sleeth | 24/7 ER Doc to 24/6 Sabbath Rest." May 5, 2020. www.graceenoughpodcast.com/67-dr-matthew-sleeth-24-7-er-doc-to-24-6-sabbath-rest.

Stern, Chaim. *Gates of Prayer: The New Union Prayerbook.* Central Conference of American Rabbis, 1975.

Swoboda, A. J. *Subversive Sabbath: The Surprising Power of Rest in a Nonstop World.* Brazos, 2018.

Taylor, Barbara Brown. *An Altar in the World: A Geography of Faith.* HarperOne, 2010.

Warren, Tish Harrison. *Liturgy of the Ordinary: Sacred Practices in Everyday Life.* InterVarsity, 2019.

Wells, John. *The Practical Sabbatarian: Or, Sabbath Holiness.* London, 1668.

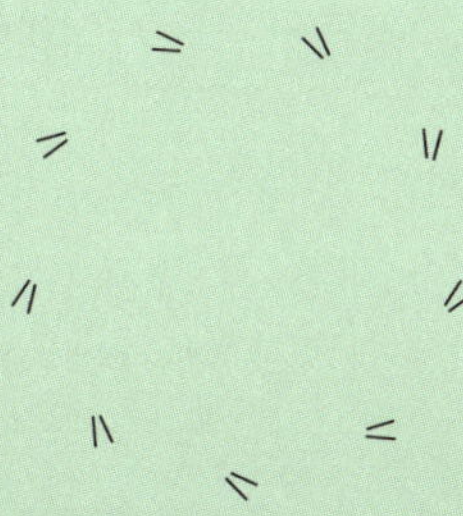

The Sabbath Practice

An ancient way to find rest for your soul

The Sabbath is a 24-hour time period set aside to stop, rest, delight, and worship. It is the best day of the week. In our era of chronic exhaustion, emotional unhealth, and spiritual stagnation, few things are more necessary than the recovery of this ancient practice.

The Practice comes with four session videos, weekly exercises and readings, and additional resources to help your group create life-changing daily rhythms as you apprentice under Jesus together. The sessions are about 30 minutes long and include time for group discussion at the beginning.

Our Practices are perfect to use with small groups or to run course-style with a larger group, but they can also be modified for a churchwide Sunday teaching series, small cohorts, and many other contexts.

To learn more, visit **practicingtheway.org/sabbath.**